Math at the Amusement Park

Representing and Solving Problems

Ian F. Mahaney

PowerKiDS press.
New York

Having math **skills** can help you everywhere. Understanding subtraction helps a person **calculate** the change returned when buying groceries. Knowing how to multiply comes in handy when you are figuring out how many batches of cookies you need to make for a bake sale.

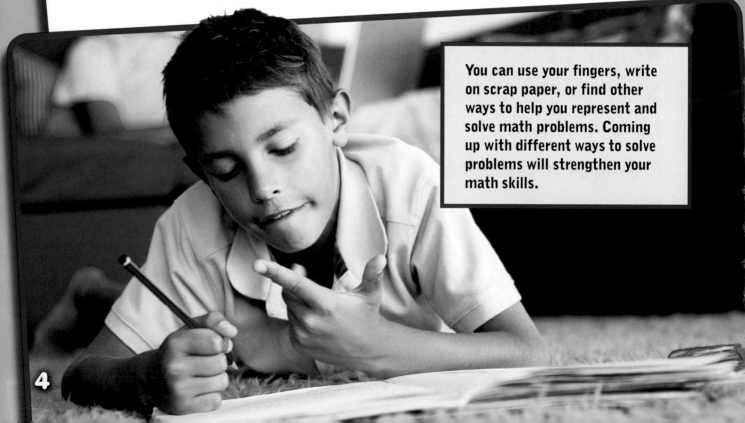

You can use your fingers, write on scrap paper, or find other ways to help you represent and solve math problems. Coming up with different ways to solve problems will strengthen your math skills.

Math helps people solve problems they come across every day. Math can even help you when you go to an amusement park. For example, if you go to the amusement park with a group in two cars, how much will it cost to park the cars? If it costs $5 to park one car, then it will cost $5 + $5 = $10 to park both cars. You just did the math you need to go have fun at the amusement park!

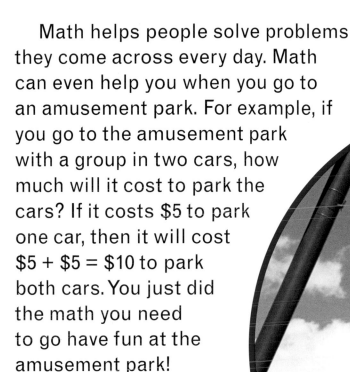

How many people are riding on this roller coaster? One way to find the answer is to multiply. You would represent the problem like this: 4 people per car x 5 cars = _____. Can you figure it out?

Figure It Out

(See answers on p. 22)

The Price of Admission

When people visit an amusement park, they have to pay **admission**. Your math skills can help you figure out how much money you need to get your group inside.

The amusement park's admission is $8, and there are four people going. You can figure out how much it costs to get in in a few ways. You can represent the problem as an addition problem: $8 + $8 + $8 + $8 = $32 for all four people to get into the park. You could also set this up as a multiplication problem: 4 people x $8 = $32 for everybody to have fun at the amusement park.

Admission is $5 and you bought 10 tickets at $2 each to go on rides. How much money did you spend? You can represent the problem this way: $5 + ($2 x 10) = $25.

Figure It Out

Your grandmother and grandfather join you at the amusement park and admission costs $6 each for seniors and $8 for everyone else. What will be the total cost for the three of you?

(See answers on p. 22)

You can use your math skills at the Ferris wheel, too. You can count the number of cars, or the **gondolas** where passengers sit. You can do problems relating to how many people fit in a car or how many cars are empty. There are so many ways to use math on the Ferris wheel!

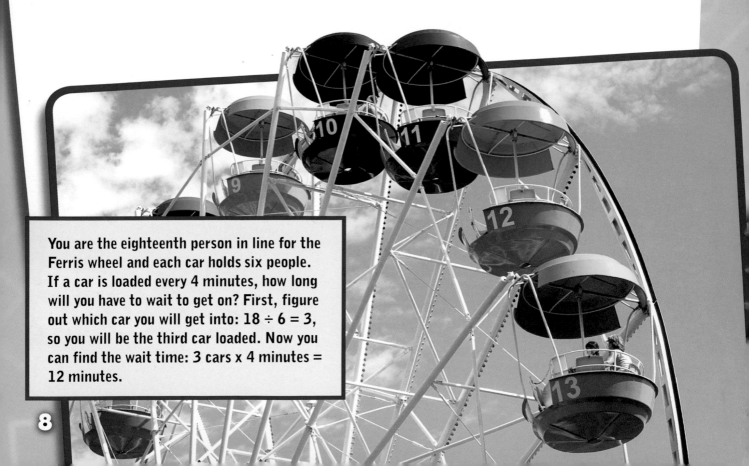

You are the eighteenth person in line for the Ferris wheel and each car holds six people. If a car is loaded every 4 minutes, how long will you have to wait to get on? First, figure out which car you will get into: 18 ÷ 6 = 3, so you will be the third car loaded. Now you can find the wait time: 3 cars x 4 minutes = 12 minutes.

The first Ferris wheel was built in 1893 and designed by George Ferris. The ride was 264 feet (80 m) tall and had 36 cars that each held 60 people. To find out how many people could ride in all, you could set up a multiplication problem: 36 cars x 60 people = 2,160 people who could ride at once.

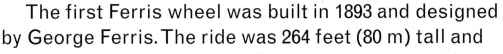

Let's say you ride a Ferris wheel that has 16 cars that hold four people each. How many people can fit on that ride?

(See answers on p. 22)

Figure It Out

Next Stop: Bumper Cars

Bumper cars are one of the few kinds of cars that kids can drive! They also allow kids a chance to show off their math skills. Pretend you are in a group of eight kids with five adults, and you are ready to drive the bumper cars.

Can you figure out how many bumper cars are needed? Two kids fit in each bumper car, so the kids will need $8 \div 2 = 4$ bumper cars. Only one adult fits in each bumper car, so the adults will need five. In total, you will need $5 + 4 = 9$ bumper cars. Now find the one you want to drive!

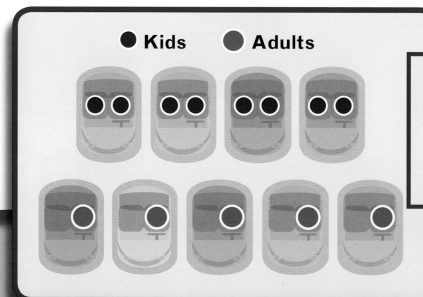

● Kids ● Adults

This diagram shows how you can visually represent the bumper car problem. You can use coins or draw circles on your paper to help you figure it out.

There's a group with three adults and six kids, and there are seven bumper cars remaining. Does everyone fit?

(See answers on p. 22)

Figure It Out

Do you like hot dogs, lemonade, and cotton candy? The **concession stand** has them. You can use math to figure out how much money you will need to buy these items. You can also figure out how much change you will receive in return for the money you give.

> If you gave the cashier $10 for two cotton candies that cost $4 in all, you will create a subtraction problem to figure out your change: $10 − $4 = $6 in change.

Let's say you buy two hot dogs that cost $3 each, two sticks of cotton candy that cost $2 each, and two lemonades that cost $2.50 each. You can figure out how much money you will need. You can represent these problems like this:

2 hot dogs = $3 + $3 = $3 x 2 = $6.
2 sticks of cotton candy = $2 x 2 = $2 + $2 = $4.
2 cups of lemonade = $2.50 x 2 = $2.50 + $2.50 = $5.
Adding it all up, you will need $6 + $4 + $5 = $15.

Figure It Out

You pay for $16 in concessions with two $10 bills. How much change will you get?

(See answers on p. 22)

Roller Coaster Math

Roller coasters are fun rides for many people. They can also be dangerous. Because of the danger, amusement parks often require roller coaster riders to be a certain height. If the **minimum** height to ride a roller coaster is 48 inches (1.2 m), how tall is that in feet? To find out, you can divide the total inches (48) by the number of inches in 1 foot (12): 48 ÷ 12 = 4 feet.

You can also use your subtraction **expertise** at the roller coaster. Let's say there are 55 people ready to ride, but 14 of them are not tall enough.

If this girl is 48 inches (1.2 m) tall, and she needs to be 52 inches (1.3 m) to go on the ride, how many inches too short is she? To figure it out, you can set up a subtraction problem: 52 inches – 48 inches = 4 inches too short.

How many still get to ride the roller coaster? You can represent this problem this way: 55 − 14 = 41 people. This tells you that 41 people will be able to ride the roller coaster.

= 55 - 14 = 41

You can use base-ten blocks to help you represent this problem. Set up blocks to show 55. Then take away 14, as is shown in red above. Count the blocks that are left to find the answer.

If a roller coaster seats two people in every row and has 40 rows, how many people can ride the roller coaster at once?

(See answers on p. 22)

Figure It Out

Step Right Up!

Many amusement parks offer carnival games. These include games in which a player throws a plastic ball into a cup or bursts a balloon with a dart to win a prize. The games are **structured** so you have to pay a small amount for one chance to win and a larger amount for many chances to win.

In a game in which players pay $1 for 1 chance to win or $5 for 10 chances, how many chances could $20 buy? Let's represent the problem using markers arranged in groups to help us solve it.

$5 = • • • • • • • • • •
$5 = • • • • • • • • • •
$5 = • • • • • • • • • •
$5 = • • • • • • • • • •

You can skip count by 5s to see how many groups of 10 you will have for $20. Then you can skip count by 10s, using the markers to help you find that $20 buys 40 chances. You can also represent the same problem this way: $20 ÷ $5 = 4 and 4 x 10 = 40, or 10 ($20 ÷ $5) = 40.

If a player has $6 to spend on this game, how many chances will she have to win a prize?

(See answers on p. 22)

Figure It Out

Line Time

Waiting in line is not fun. Sometimes to have fun at an amusement park, though, you have to wait in line. You can use your math skills to see how much time you spend waiting. Then you have to decide if the wait is worth your time.

Let's say you waited 10 minutes to pay for admission, 15 minutes for the Ferris wheel, 10 minutes at the bumper cars, 5 minutes to buy concessions, and 30 minutes to ride the roller coaster. We can solve this by setting it up as an addition problem: $10 + 15 + 10 + 5 + 30 = 70$ minutes. There are 60 minutes in an hour, so that is 1 hour and 10 minutes. That is a lot of waiting!

A boy visits an amusement park and drives the bumper cars twice. He waits in line 3 minutes the first time and 11 minutes the second time. The ride lasts 6 minutes. Did the boy drive the bumper cars or wait in line longer?

(See answers on p. 22)

Figure It Out

19

There is a lot more math you can use at an amusement park. You can describe the shapes of the rides. You need to add, multiply, subtract, and divide when you pay for tickets, buy snacks, or break up your group to fit on the rides.

There is even math in the parking lot! If the **capacity** of an amusement park is 6,000 people, how many parking spots are needed? If everyone drives alone, it would be 6,000. Normally, though, people visit in groups. If the amusement park learns that visitors come in groups of three, then the amusement park needs $6,000 \div 3 = 2,000$ parking spots. Can you think of other math used in an amusement park?

Next time you are at an amusement park, think about all the times you use math while you are there. Math does not get much more fun than that!

If 6,000 people visit the amusement park, and they all come in groups of four people to a car, how many cars would there be in the parking lot?

(See answers on p. 22)

Figure It Out

Figure It Out: The Answers

Page 5: There are 20 people riding this roller coaster.

Page 7: Your grandparents are charged $6 each ($6 + $6). You are charged $8 to enter. The total cost is $6 + $6 + $8 = $20.

Page 9: This Ferris wheel holds 16 x 4 = 64 people.

Page 11: The group will need 3 bumper cars for the adults and 6 ÷ 2 = 3 bumper cars for the kids. The group will need 3 + 3 = 6 bumper cars. Since 7 bumper cars are available, yes, everybody fits.

Page 13: The money you paid is $10 + $10 = $20. The concessions cost $16. Your change is the difference, $20 − $16 = $4.

Page 15: The roller coaster seats 40 x 2 = 80 people.

Page 17: She will have 10 chances for $5 and $1 left over to buy 1 chance. In total, she will have 10 + 1 = 11 chances to win a prize.

Page 19: The boy waits in line 3 minutes + 11 minutes = 14 minutes. The rides last 6 minutes x 2 rides = 12 minutes. Since 14 minutes > 12 minutes, the boy waits in line longer than the rides last.

Page 21: The number of cars in the parking lot is 6,000 ÷ 4 = 1,500 cars.

Glossary

admission (ud-MIH-shun) The cost to enter.

calculate (KAL-kyuh-layt) To figure out with math.

capacity (kuh-PA-sih-tee) The total amount that someone or something can make or hold.

concession stand (kun-SEH-shun STAND) A place to buy snacks.

expertise (ek-spur-TEEZ) Knowledge.

gondolas (GON-duh-luz) Cars that people ride in on a Ferris wheel.

minimum (MIH-nih-mum) The smallest amount accepted.

skills (SKILZ) Abilities or things that help one do a job well.

structured (STRUK-churd) Made or organized.

Index

A
adult(s), 10–11, 22

C
car(s), 5, 8–11, 18–19, 22
change, 4, 12–13, 22
concessions, 13, 18, 22
cost, 7, 22
cotton candy, 12–13

D
danger, 14

F
fun, 5–6, 18

G
game(s), 16–17
groceries, 4
group(s), 5–6, 10–11, 16, 20, 22

H
height, 14
hot dogs, 12–13

K
kids, 10–11, 22
kinds, 10

L
lemonade(s), 12–13

M
money, 6, 12–13, 22

P
passengers, 8
person, 4–6, 8–9, 14–15, 20–22

R
ride(s), 9, 14, 19–22
roller coaster(s), 5, 14–15, 18, 22

S
seniors, 7
subtraction, 4, 14

Websites

Due to the changing nature of Internet links, PowerKids Press has developed an online list of websites related to the subject of this book. This site is updated regularly. Please use this link to access the list:
www.powerkidslinks.com/cms/amuse/